THE
JACOBITE RE
IN LANCASHIRE

by

Jane Sterling

DALESMAN BOOKS
1973

20p

The Dalesman Publishing Company Limited
Clapham (via Lancaster)
Yorkshire

First published 1973

ISBN: 0 85206 180 3

The cover illustration and the title page sketch are by E. Jeffrey. Photographs by the author. The extract from 'Devil Water' by Anya Seton is by permission of Messrs. Hodder and Stoughton.

Hortus Printing Co. Ltd., Burnley, Lancs.

1 The Jacobite Rising of 1715

THE Commonwealth period which followed the Civil Wars temporarily put an end to the hopes of the Stuarts. Oliver Cromwell ruled the country until his death in 1658 when he was for a short time succeeded by his son Richard. By this time most of the people of England had had enough of rule by the army and the Puritans, and there was widespread rejoicing when the exiled son of the executed Charles I returned to his homeland in 1660 to reign as Charles II. Once again England was to be ruled by a king – though by a king whose power was no longer that absolute power which his predecessors had claimed. The restored king could only make laws and levy taxes with the consent of Parliament. Not only the monarchy but the Anglican Church was restored in 1660. This was another popular move as many people had become weary of the narrow-minded and strait-laced Puritans. Puritans who had held high offices had to choose between their position and their religion for after 1660 Anglicans held all the most important positions in the country.

Charles himself was an Anglican of course. He married a Roman Catholic but as his wife produced no heir to the throne he was likely to be succeeded by his brother James, an Anglican married to an Anglican wife. James had two daughters, Mary and Anne, both brought up in the Protestant faith. The Anglican succession seemed secure. But after the death of his first wife James married again – this time the Roman Catholic Mary of Modena. James himself had strong leanings towards Roman Catholicism and in 1676 he forsook the Anglican religion and joined the Church of Rome. There was consternation among Anglicans in high places who had no wish to be superseded in the next reign by Roman Catholics and there was fear, too, among those in lowly places who were apprehensive about what the consequences of the change might be. Attempts were made to debar James from the throne, but they came to nothing, and when that merry monarch Charles II died in 1685 his brother succeeded him as James II.

So long as James and his second wife had no children, and Mary, married to the Protestant William of Orange, was heiress to the throne, there was no possibility of a Roman Catholic dynasty being founded to rule England. It was the birth of a son to Mary of Modena that caused a crisis. This boy, born to James and Mary after seventeen years of marriage, would be brought up as a Roman Catholic and he would be the next king of England. Now the remote possibility of a line of Roman Catholic kings had become a probability – and a probability that would not be tolerated by Parliament or by the majority of the people. So in 1688 Parliament invited James' Protestant daughter Mary and her husband to come to England to reign jointly as king and queen. James II fled to the Continent and lived in exile for the rest of his life.

The events of 1688 and 1689 which deposed James and brought William and Mary to reign in his stead are known as the Bloodless or Glorious Revolution. Revolution it certainly was for it made vital differences in the government of this country. William and Mary reigned by invitation of Parliament; there was now no question that they were monarchs by Divine Right. People and Parliament had shown that they could remove and create kings – henceforth power was fundamentally vested in Parliament, not in the monarchy.

There were, however, many who did not accept the revolution settlement. Most of those who would have preferred James Stuart to have remained king were Roman Catholics of whom there were still a great number in Lancashire. Many of the most important families there would have been glad to see James restored and were willing to support plans for the overthrow of the Revolution Settlement. The supporters of the exiled James came to be known as Jacobites. (The name comes from Jacobus, the Latin form of the name James.)

James lived in exile in France during the reign of Louis XIV, the life-long enemy of William of Orange, ruler of Holland, who had, as a result of the 1688–9 revolution, also become king of England. The king of France had found it easy to dominate England's foreign policy while the Stuart kings reigned in England, but now that France's enemy William was king of our country English armies and ships would be used against "The Sun King." Therefore it suited Louis' purposes to support the Jacobites for two main reasons. If the Jacobites were successful as a result of French help the restored Stuarts would be friendly towards France and, secondly, while Louis was known to support the Jacobites, England would never be safe from invasion and William would have to keep some of his soldiers in readiness for an attack. Thus, William could not muster his total forces for theatres of war in Europe and was compelled to keep a strict vigilance for signs of rebellion in his new country.

The first serious menace to William's position came during

the early years of his reign. James II, supported by Louis XIV, landed in Ireland as a first step towards recovering his throne. The Irish, who had suffered terrible privations during the Protestant rule of Cromwell, welcomed James and soon his forces controlled nearly all Ireland. William sent a strong army via Lancashire to Ireland and James' forces were overwhelmingly defeated at the Battle of the Boyne on July 12th, 1691. James was forced to take refuge with his French friends once again.

Before and during the campaign in Ireland there had been great activity among Lancashire Jacobites. There is no doubt that if James had been able to establish himself securely in Ireland his forces would have made their first landing in England on the Lancashire coast. Secret plans had been worked out for this and help was ready. Two Roman Catholics, Lunt and Threlfall, had been brought secretly to Lancashire and landed at Cockerham on the Fylde coast to prepare the way for invasion. Just as many of the old-established families of Lancashire had been willing to risk their lives for the sake of their king during the Civil War, so their descendants were willing to wager their position and fortune to support the beheaded king's son to regain the throne. The two undercover agents, Lunt and Threlfall, offered the Lancashire Jacobite gentry commissions signed by James II to serve as officers when the Jacobites landed in Lancashire. But all the plots came to nothing for, as we have seen, James was defeated at the Battle of the Boyne, and the conspiracies in Lancashire were discovered and ended in a sensational trial which took place in Manchester when eight Lancashire landowners – including Lord Molyneux of Sefton – were accused of treason. The surprising thing was that in spite of evidence against them they were all acquitted. Jacobite activity died down when peace was made between Louis XIV and William. Without financial support from France the Jacobites dared not openly resist the Revolution Settlement.

Mary and William continued to rule jointly until Mary died. Then William reigned as sole monarch until 1702 when the king who had defied the mighty strength of Louis XIV, the most powerful monarch in Europe, was killed by "a little gentleman in black velvet" – a mole! While William was out riding one morning his horse Sorrell stumbled on a mole hill and threw his royal rider who died as a result of his injuries.

Mary's sister, Anne, the second daughter of James II, became queen when William died. Though Anne had seventeen children not one of them lived to survive her and when she died the crown passed, not to her half-brother James (son of James II and Mary of Modena) who had been debarred from inheriting

The Stork at Conder Green. Formerly known as Ye Fighting Cocks, this old inn was a rendezvous for Jacobite conspirators.

the throne, but to a distant Protestant relative, George, the Elector of Hanover, who on Anne's death in 1714 was proclaimed George I of England.

George I, a great grandson of James I, was not an attractive character. He couldn't speak a word of English, so it is not surprising that he was greeted with no great enthusiasm in England. Many romantically-minded English and a great many Scots were more attracted to the exiled Stuarts. James II was by this time dead and the Stuart claims vested in the person of his son, known as James III to his supporters, and now usually referred to as "The Old Pretender." There was a great uprising of Jacobite feeling in the north, and under the cover of social gatherings Jacobite conspirators met together. At functions all over Lancashire the Jacobite sympathisers showed their true feelings whenever they drank the health of the king. As they raised their glasses they passed them over their finger bowls to show that though they were drinking a loyal toast it was to the king over the water – the exiled James III. This idea was echoed in one of the favourite ditties of the time, said to have been written by a Lancashire man, John Byrom:

The Old Dog Lad stone at Myerscough Lodge, now part of the Lancashire College of Agriculture (see page 9).

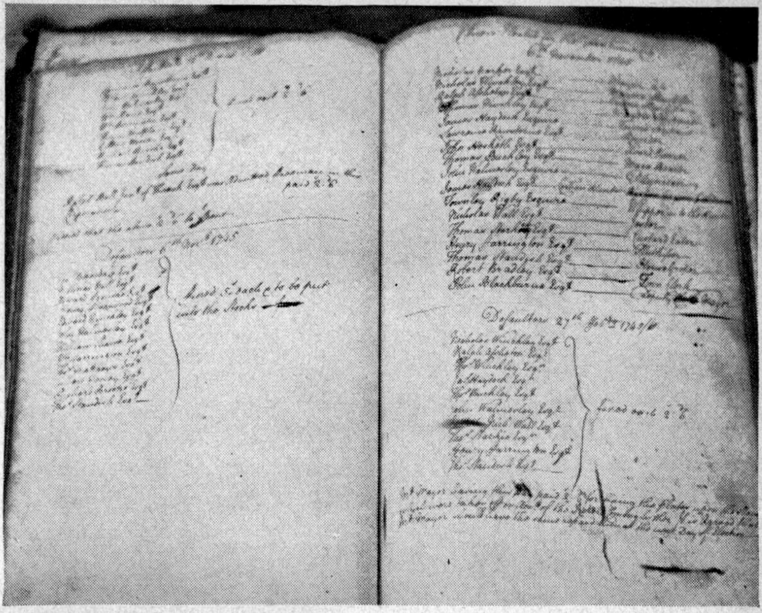

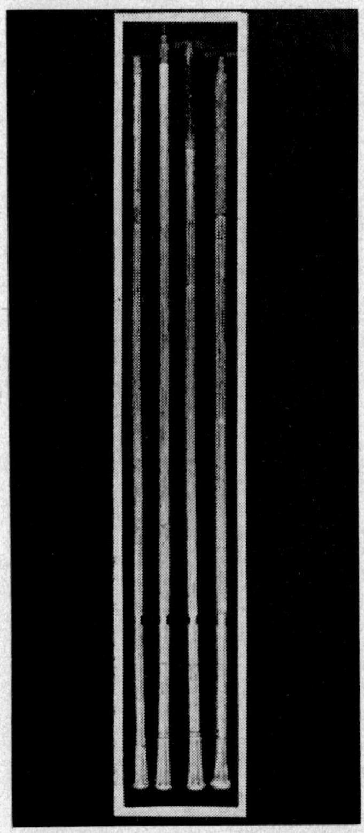

Relics of the Mock Corporation of Walton-le-Dale. Above: Pages from the Corporation's records. Left: These four silver staves, part of the Corporation's regalia, are inscribed with the names of members, many of whom fought for the Jacobite cause. (Photographs by permission of the curator of the Harris Museum, Preston.)

THE JACOBITE RISING OF 1715

God bless the King, I mean our Faith's Defender,
God bless, no harm in blessing, the Pretender,
But who Pretender is, and who is King,
God bless us all, that's quite another thing.

Many of the old inns of Lancashire have seen secret meetings of the Jacobites. One which Kathleen Fidler features in her children's book *Lanterns over the Lune* is now called The Stork at Conder Green, near Glasson Dock. Formerly known as Ye Fighting Cocks, it is believed to have been a meeting place for Jacobites planning the restoration of the Stuarts. Another is the Foxhall Hotel on the promenade at Blackpool. This was formerly the private residence of Edward Tyldesley and a secret room was prepared there ready to hide James III when he returned to England. Tyldesley, the grandson of Thomas Tyldesley who died for the Stuart cause at the Battle of Wigan Lane in 1651, kept a diary which covers the years 1712–4, and in it are mentioned many of the Lancashire gentry who became involved in the Jacobite rebellions. Edward Tyldesley was also the owner of Myerscough Hall, now part of the Lancashire County College of Agriculture. Still preserved there is a memorial stone to the "Old Dog Lad." In her book Kathleen Fidler interprets this odd inscription as the name that Tyldesley used in his role as one of the chief Jacobite agents in the county – a role that was later taken over by John Dalton of Thurnham Hall.

The Unicorn Inn at Walton-le-Dale (now a café) was one of the most interesting of the inns associated with the Jacobites. There, during the 18th century, meetings of the mock corporation of Walton-le-Dale were held. The corporation appointed its own officials – the usual town dignitaries such as a mayor and town clerk, and some strange-sounding officers with names like custard-eater and slut-kisser! The corporation had its own regalia – a mace, silver staves, halberds, etc. – some of which, together with records of the meetings of the corporation, can still be seen at the Harris Museum in Preston. Although on the surface the corporation existed only to poke fun at the Hanoverian-supporting real mayor and corporation of Preston, in fact its members were all staunch Jacobites and it is probable that behind the frivolity of the feastings and meetings was the earnest business of organising plots for the overthrow of George I and the restoration of the Stuarts.

Feelings of discontent and hatred of the lethargic German-speaking George I eventually found expression in risings in Lancashire and in other parts of the country. In Manchester the Jacobites (mostly Roman Catholic supporters) rose against the Protestant settlement and took vengeance on the Presbyterian chapel in Cross Street, which they set on fire. An isolated

Skerton Bridge, Lancaster. Built by Thomas Harrison in the 1780s, it replaced the old bridge damaged by attempts to frustrate the Jacobite's march into Lancaster.

outbreak like this was easily subdued by Government troops. The rebels were sent to Lancaster, where they were imprisoned and made to stand in the pillory. An eye-witness who saw them there reports, "I was at Lancaster and saw them stand in the pillory there which was on a Saturday . . . but no person was allowed to fling anything at them." Another outbreak of violence at Warrington was ended as speedily.

The most important rising which led to the famous Jacobite rebellion of 1715 started in Scotland, where the Earl of Marr rallied the Stuart supporters in the Highlands. All over the north of England long-made plans were put into action and an army (to support the Scottish rebels) was raised by the Earl of Derwentwater, who lived at Dilston in Northumberland. The earl, who in 1701 had been a distinguished member of the mock corporation of Walton-le-Dale, was in close touch with the many Jacobites in Lancashire. Another of the leaders of the rebellion, Lord Widdrington, was connected by marriage with the Towneleys of Towneley Hall near Burnley. On a recruiting campaign for support for the rebellion in Lancashire he had been promised "that immediately upon the Scottish force making its appearance in Lancashire there would be a general insurrection of at least 20,000 men." Because of this, after the Earl of Derwentwater's forces joined the Scottish force at Kelso the combined army of about 1,700 men marched south through Cumberland to Lancashire, and made their way towards the ancient county town of Lancaster. Some support was forthcoming. The Jacobites were joined by many local gentlemen, including John Dalton of Thurnham, Ralph Standish from Borwick, Edward Tyldesley of Myerscough, Albert Hodgson the owner of Leighton Hall and Richard Butler of Rawcliffe Hall, but they were disappointed in their expectation of the promised "20,000 men."

Resistance to the rebels was organised by Sir Henry Hoghton of Hoghton Tower and the local Hanoverian, Colonel Charteris, who lived at Hornby Castle. Charteris was well known to the Scots and had a bad reputation. He had been dismissed from the English army serving in Europe, had fled to Scotland and managed to secure a commission as colonel in charge of a cavalry regiment. North of the border, Charteris made a fortune by cheating at cards and when news that he had been dismissed from the English army reached Scotland he had to leave hastily. In London he amassed more wealth by charging extortionate interest on money loans. Eventually he bought Hornby Castle for £14,500 and settled there. For a man who lived by his wits he did not prove a brilliant tactician in war. As the Jacobites advanced towards Lancaster it was Colonel Charteris who suggested that, to stop their progress, the bridge over the Lune should be blown up. After work had started on this project the tide went out – to show that the advancing Highlanders could ford the river without any difficulty!

On November 7th, 1715, the Jacobite army crossed the bridge into Lancaster. An eye-witness account of their entry "with swords drawn, drums beating and colours flying" is contained in the diary of Peter Clarke, a lawyer's clerk from Kendal who wrote *A Journal of Severall Occurences from 2nd November 1715 In the Insurrection Began in Scotland and Concluded at Preston in Lancashire* – a fascinating contemporary account of the rebellion. According to this authority the rebels marched straight to the Market Place where the Old Pretender was proclaimed as King James III. One who watched the proceedings with more than a casual interest was Christopher Hopkin, a stationer, who was arrested by order of Thomas Forster for spying on the Jacobites and "taking account of the number of them."

Prisoners released from Lancaster Castle by the insurgents included Thomas Siddall, who had been imprisoned for his

part in the Manchester riots. The next task of the rebel army was to scour the town for weapons and gunpowder. All houses were searched if the residents did not give up their arms voluntarily, but no gunpowder was found. The only man who had a supply, one Samuel Satterthwaite, had thrown the lot into the town well, of all places, reputedly on the advice of Colonel Charteris.

While this search was going on another group of the rebels was sent to Sunderland Point. Nowadays Sunderland Point is a lonely hamlet at the mouth of the River Lune cut off from civilisation when the high tides swirl between it and the rest of the Lune Valley, but in the early 18th century it was a busy and thriving port built up as a result of the enterprise of a Quaker merchant, Robert Lawson. His ships traded in timber, cotton and other goods and his house and warehouses still remain to testify to the one-time prosperity of this forgotten port. In November 1715, when the Jacobites marched to Lancaster, Robert Lawson had anchored at Sunderland Point a ship with six cannon and some small arms on board. Charteris and Hoghton had tried to buy the guns from Robert Lawson but their efforts had been unsuccessful. Lawson refused to sell unless he was promised a bond of £10,000 to cover him against any damage the Jacobites might do to his goods or ships if they found out that he had sold his guns to Government

Buildings with Jacobite associations. Left: Robert Lawson's house at Sunderland Point. Above: Thurnham Hall, rebuilt in the 19th century, was the home of John Dalton, one of the leaders of the Lancashire Jacobites.

officers. The bond was refused, so Lawson refused to sell his guns. He was then ordered to moor his ship out of reach of the Jacobites, but he had obviously taken no notice of this command as the rebels were easily able to take the guns from Robert Lawson's ship.

The next day, November 8th, a service was held in St. Mary's priory church at Lancaster. An engineer called Mr. Ginn had done a speedy job on the new prayer book, erased the name of George I from the prayer for the royal family and inserted in its place the name of James III. A Jacobite who saw the altered prayer book declared, "The said words are writ with such a nicety that many take them to have been printed." The service was conducted by the Rev. William Paul, a Jacobite minister, and the congregation "gay with the uniforms of the soldiers and the bright colours worn by the many ladies present, prayed, or seemed to pray, with fervour for his Majesty King James III."

The Highland officers seem to have made a great impression on the ladies of Lancaster. Peter Clarke wrote, "This afternoon the gentlemen soldiers dressed and trimmed themselves up in

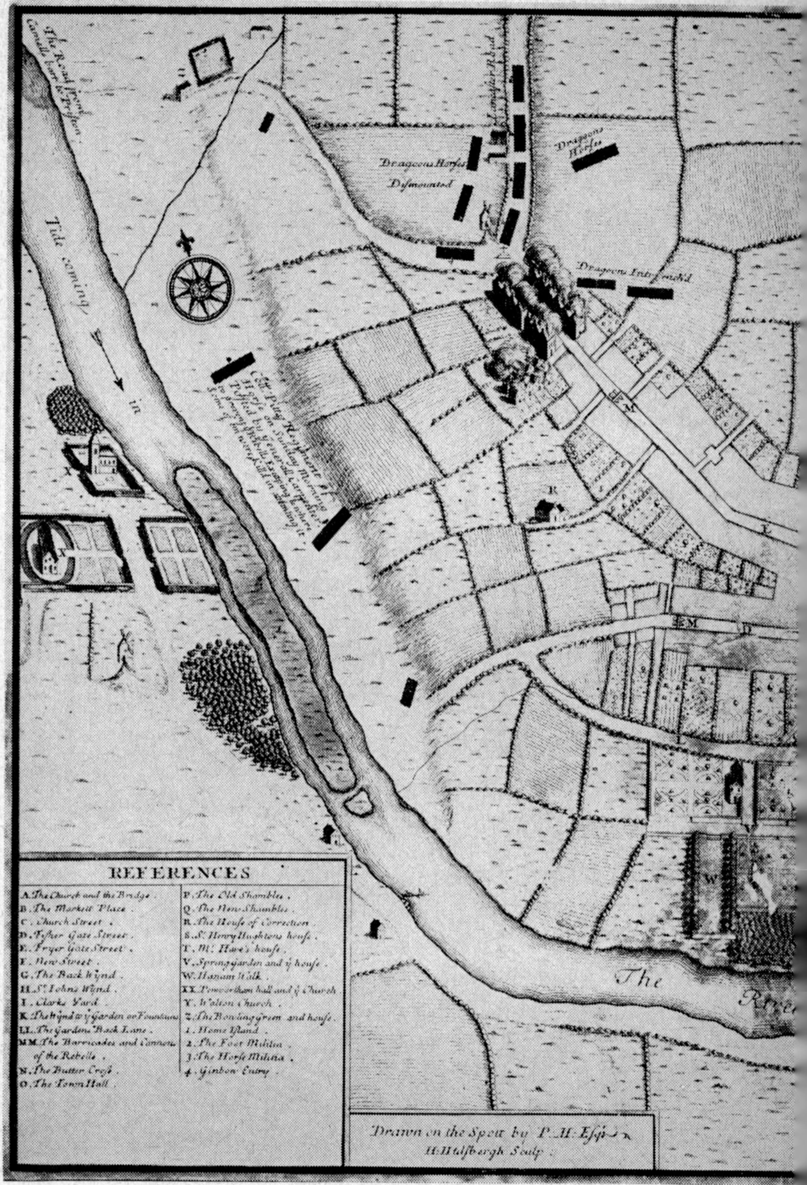
Tide coming in
Dragoons Horses Dismounted
Dragoons Horses
Dragoons Intrench'd
The River
REFERENCES
A. The Church and the Bridge.
B. The Markett Place.
C. Church Street.
D. Fisher Gate Street.
E. Fryer Gate Street.
F. New Street.
G. The Back Wynd.
H. St. Johns Wynd.
I. Clarks Yard.
K. The Wynd w y Garden or Fountains
LL. The Gardens Back Lane.
MM. The Barricades and Cannon of the Rebells.
N. The Butter Cross.
O. The Town Hall.
P. The Old Shambles.
Q. The New Shambles.
R. The House of Correction.
S. Sr. Henry Hughtons house.
T. Mr. Hare's house.
V. Springgarden and y house.
W. Hanam Walk.
XX. Penwortham hall and y Church.
Y. Walton Church.
Z. The Bowlinggreen and house.
1. Home Island.
2. The Foot Militia.
3. The Horse Militia.
4. Ginbow Entry.
Drawn on the Spott by P. H. Esqr.
H. Hulsbergh Sculp.

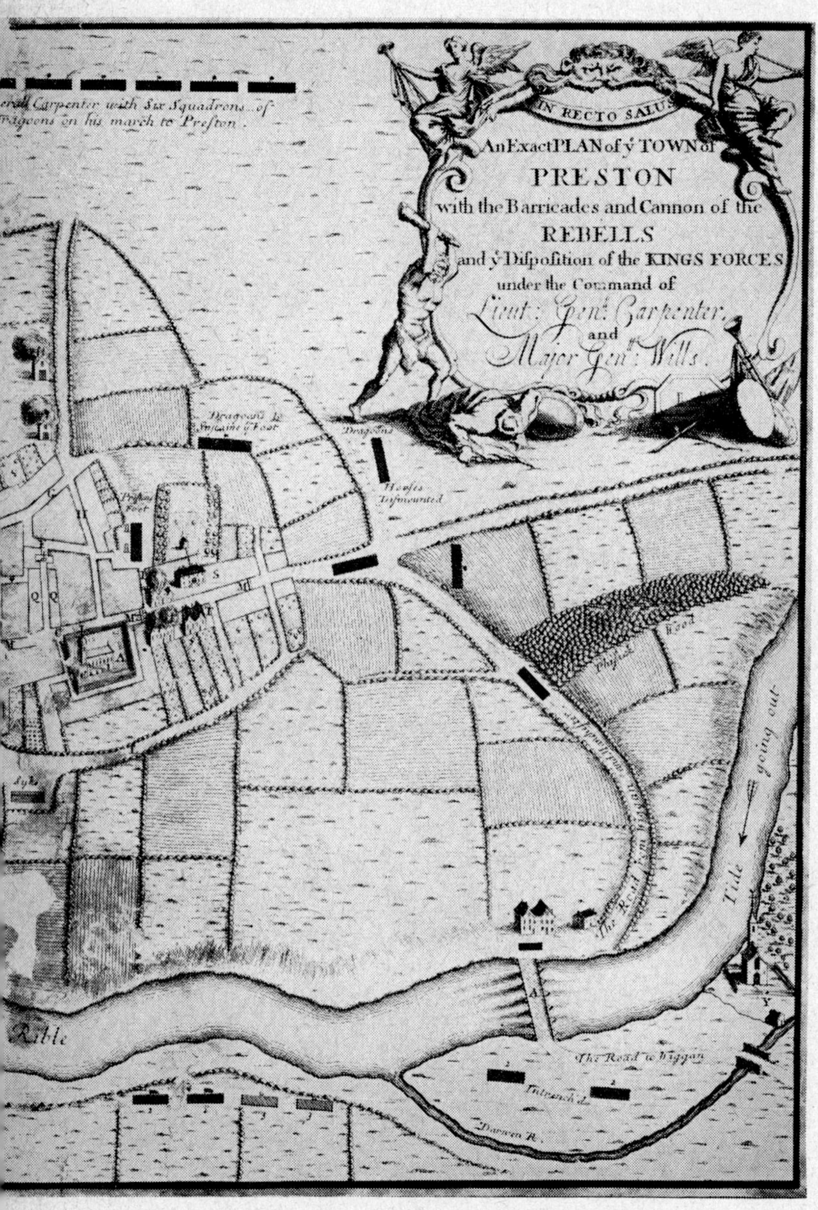

A plan of the Battle of Preston, fought in November, 1715.
(By courtesy of the Lancashire Records Office.)

their best cloathes for to drink a dish of tea with the ladys of this towne. The ladys also appeared in their best riging and had their teatables richly furnished for to entertain their new suitors." On both nights of the Jacobites' stay in Lancaster, balls were held and many Lancashire ladies lost their hearts to the gallant handsome Jacobite officers. Peter Clarke says that when the army moved off towards Preston they were very sorrowful to part with their "new loves." But if many of the ladies of Lancaster were reluctant to see the rebels move on, there were others like the stolid Quaker merchant, William Stout, who were glad to see the Jacobites depart and leave Lancaster to its busy but peaceful commercial life again. In his diary William Stout records his impressions: "It was a time of trial and fear that the Scots and northern rebels would have plundered us, but they were very civil, and to most paid for what they had."

On November 9th the Jacobite army moved off from Lancaster in good spirits with the guns taken from Robert Lawson's ship and part of a large consignment of brandy seized from the Customs House, for on November 8th, according to Peter Clarke:

"Also this day Commissioners were appointed to examine the books belonging to the Customs House here, but found nothing due to the crown, only a part of a large quantity of brandy which the Customs House officers had some days before seized, being run from the Isle of Man. The said officers had made use of a small part of it, and the new Commissioners took possession of the remainder part, some of which they drank in this town, and the rest they carried away in a cart towards Garstang, but they made an end of it before they came to that town."

The foot soldiers marched as far as Garstang, where they stayed the night. The cavalry pressed on to Preston where "the foot coming up the next day they marched straight up to the cross and they were drawn up as usual while the Pretender was proclaimed." In her book *Devil Water*, an exciting historical novel about the Earl of Derwentwater and his family, Anya Seton describes the scene in the market place at Preston on that November day: "The different troops arranged themselves neatly, headed by their mounted officers, and radiating like spokes of a wheel from the central market cross. On the steps stood the herald with his trumpet. Beside him General Foster, in scarlet and gold on his huge black horse. Smiling citizens were jammed in every window of the neat brick mansions and the half-timbered shops. They cheered as the square filled with mounted gentlemen in laced hats all garnished with the white cockade (the emblem of the Jacobites), in full-bottomed wigs, ruffles and flashing scabbards. They gawked at the company of Highlanders with their sporrans, their gaudy tartan breeches and plaids, their flopping bonnets, the like of which Preston had never seen.

"There was a preliminary roll of drums, the skirling of bagpipes, then a hush as the herald blew his trumpet and began to shout the proclamation. 'Whereas George, Elector of Brunswick, has usurped and taken upon him the style of King of these realms . . . and whereas James the Third by Reason of the Right of the First-born son and the laws of this land, did immediately after his father's decease become our only and lawful liege . . .'

"James (the Earl of Derwentwater) listened attentively as he always did, and his heart was suddenly lightened while the herald finished and the Stuart standard was run up on the pole prepared for it. He stared at the great green taffeta flag with its creamy fringe and lavishly embroidered emblem of charity – a pelican feeding her young. As James and all the hundreds in the crowded square uncovered their heads, brilliant sunshine gilded the flag which rippled proudly, in a breeze from the sea. 'God Save the King' came the thunderous acclaim. It echoed down the crowded streets and rang from the windows of the surrounding houses."

In Preston the Jacobite army was reinforced by more of the local gentry with their tenants, but the total strength of the force was still no more than 4,000 men at the most. As at Lancaster, so at Preston the Jacobites found the ladies enchanting. Peter Clarke records in his diary, "The ladys in this town are so very beautiful, and so richly attired that the gentlemen soldiers from Wednesday to Saturday minded nothing but courting and feasting." It was these three days of carefree gaiety which led to the downfall of the Jacobite army. As they drank, danced and made merry they gave the government time to organise their forces. By Saturday, November 12th, two armies were converging on the Jacobites at Preston. General Carpenter had been sent to Northumberland to deal with the insurgents but they had moved off before he had reached them. Following the Jacobite army he now approached Preston from the Ribble Valley. Another army under General Wills approached Preston from the south. Henry Hoghton was busy organising local resistance to help the trained soldiers. In a letter to the minister of the Presbyterian Church at Chowbent, written the day before the Battle of Preston began, he says:

"The officers here (at Wigan) design to march at break of day for Preston. They have desired me to raise what men I can to meet us at Preston tomorrow, so desire you to raise all the force you can, I mean lusty young fellows to draw up on Cuerdon Green, to be there by 10 o'clock, to bring with them what armes they have fitt for service, and scythes put in straight polls, and such as have not, to bring spades and billhooks for pioneering with. Pray go immediately all amongst your neighbours and give this notice.

I am your very faithful servant,

H. Hoghton."

On the Saturday morning, General Wills with two regiments of dragoons and the militia raised by Henry Hoghton approached Preston from Wigan and surprised the Jacobites who were completely unaware of imminent danger. Reports that Government troops had been mustered at Wigan had been ignored by General Forster, appointed by the Earl of Derwentwater to command the English Jacobites. Forster, who proved useless as a military leader, refused to admit the possibility of attack until troops were actually seen approaching Preston. It was decided, probably on the advice of Brigadier Mackintoch who was in charge of the Highlanders, to withdraw the troops defending Walton Bridge and to concentrate on the defence of the town centre and its approaches. Consequently, barricades were rapidly constructed from anything the Jacobites could lay their hands on: furniture, sacks, beds, etc., were all piled high to stop the approach of General Wills' troops. The plan reproduced on page 14 shows the positions of the barricades.

General Wills crossed Walton Bridge and deployed his men to attack the barricades and to block the exits from the town. The day's fighting at the Church Street barricade where the Earl of Derwentwater was in charge is summed up by Peter Clarke: "About two o'clock this afternoon two hundred of General Wills' men entered the Churchgate Street, and the Highlanders firing out of cellars and windows in ten minutes time killed a hundred and twenty of them. The Highlanders also fired the said two ship guns (brought from Sunderland Point) but the bullets flew upon the houses, so that no execution was done thereby."

Apart from the withdrawal from two houses which afforded vantage points, the Jacobites were everywhere victorious. They gave no ground and inflicted heavy losses on the Government forces. Even a Hanoverian had to admit "the rebels seem to have had some advantage, having repulsed the King's forces in all their attacks, and maintained their posts."

But the jubilation of the Jacobites on the success of the first day's fighting was short-lived. Without effective leadership their cause was lost. By next morning, after a night when "both armies lay upon their arms but General Forster went to bed," Wills' troops were joined by Carpenter's army. The Jacobites were surrounded by forces far superior to their own. Escape was impossible and when General Forster was finally roused from his bed he was willing to ask for immediate surrender terms. The Highland soldiers were appalled at the thought of giving up the struggle and were determined to fight to the end. Confusion and chaos reigned among the Jacobites as more Government troops entered the town. There was no real battle but many skirmishes between the two sides and buildings were set on fire. General Wills promised that if the Jacobites would surrender he would "prevent his soldiers hacking them to pieces" and spare their lives until he had further orders.

So in the Preston market place, where only a few days earlier the Jacobites had confidently proclaimed James III as their rightful king, they surrendered their weapons and themselves to the army of the hated George I. In his journal Peter Clarke records the plundering that Preston suffered at the hands of the victorious troops of Generals Wills and Carpenter: "After the two said Generals' men had taken possession of the said town of Preston, they with force and armes broke open doors and locks of chambers and closets, and moneys, plate, goods and chatels of most of the inhabitants of that town (who were and still are good subjects to His Majesty King George's Government) contrary to the will of the owners of the said goods feloniously did steal, take and carry away contrary to his said Majesty's peace, crown and dignity, and also contrary to the laws of this nation in that case made and provided."

More than fifteen hundred Jacobite prisoners were taken. The officers were held in three inns near the market place – the Mitre, the Windmill and the White Bull. The rank and file of the insurgent army were rounded up and marched to the parish church, where a strong guard of Government troops was mounted over them. They were fed on rations of bread and water and the people of Preston complained of having to supply even such meagre necessities. A historian of the rebellion describes the miserable condition of these prisoners who had marched to Preston with high hopes, and now had time to regret their folly: "It was an unreasonable time of the year for imprisonment within the cold and cheerless aisles of a church, which caused the hapless captives to seek for additional protection from the inclemencies of a November month by ripping the linings from the seats or pews for additional clothing." About four hundred prisoners went from the freezing aisles of Preston church to the wretched cold stables at Lancaster Castle where "the ladies of the town thought it expedient to ignore their former friends, when they fell into adversity."

The diary of William Stout, the Quaker merchant of Lancaster, provides details of the sojourn of the prisoners in

Lancaster Castle as well as interesting information about some financial benefits to the shopkeepers of the town. His journal for 1716 records: "Last year and this was a time of much trouble and danger, on account of the Rebelion, in which we were in feare of being plundered or worse, but Almighty Providence preserved us. After the Rebelion at Preston was supressed, about fower hundred of them were brought to Lancaster Castell, and a regiment of dragoons quartred in the town to gard them. The King allowed them each fower pence a day in maintenance, viz 2d in bread, 1d in cheese, and 1d in small beer; and they laid in straw in the stables, most of them. And in a months time, about one hundred of them were conveighed to Liverpoole to be tryed, where they were convicted, and near 40 of them hanged at Manchester, Liverpoole, Wiggan, Preston, Garsting and Lancaster. And about two hundred of them continued a year and about 50 of them died and the rest were transported to America; . . . Whilst they were here I was imployed to buy cheese for them, about 2 or 3 hundred weight a week, of about 12 or 14s a hundred (weight). Besids the King's allowance, they had supplys privetly from the Papists and dis-afected to as to live very plentyfully. This year provisions were plenty and cheap, as also corn and hay, and although a regiment of dragoons was quartered here all the winter, hay was as cheape at ye spring as at the fale. And although it was hard upon innkeepers, it was a profit to the country, and it was compuited that the dragoons' and prisoners' maintainance this year amounted to at least three thousand pounds."

As Stout records, most prisoners were tried at Liverpool. The trials began on January 20th and by February 9th 74 prisoners had been sentenced. Altogether 24 Lancashire rebels were sentenced to death and their executions took place in widely separated parts of the county so that as many people as possible would hear about and evidence what happened to those who tried to displant the Hanoverians as kings of England. Of those who died twelve were hanged at Preston, four at Lancaster, where their heads were impaled on the castle gate-way, four at Garstang, seven at Wigan, five at Manchester and four at Liverpool. The sheriff's accounts for these executions make gruesome reading and include such items as: "January 27th – Erecting gallows and paid for materialls, hurdles, fire, cart, etc., in exciting Shuttleworth and four more at Preston and setting up his head on a pole in front of the Town Hall . . . £12 – 0 – 4d."

The cords used to pinion the prisoners cost 2s. 6d. Altogether the two executioners appointed for carrying out the death sentences on the prisoners were paid £60 and their travelling expenses amounted to £7 – 10 – 0d.

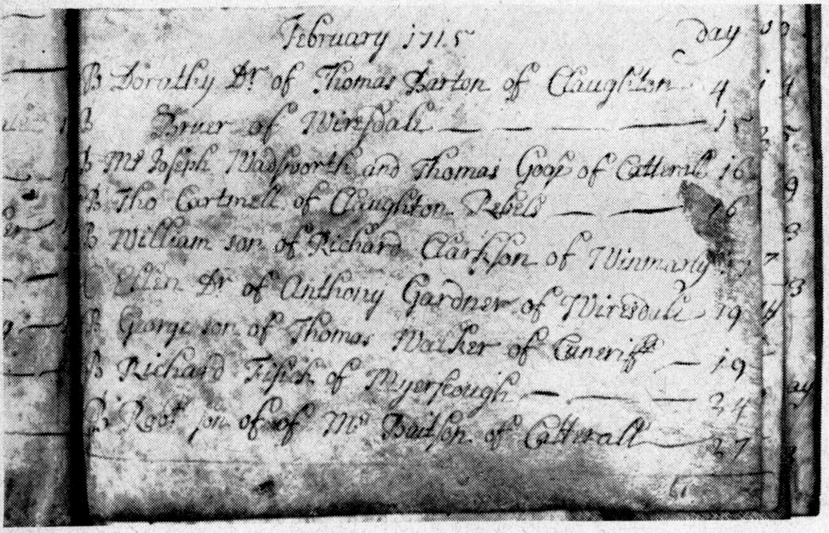
February 1715 day
B Dorothy Dr of Thomas Barton of Claughton 4
B [illegible] Bruer of Wiresdale 15
B Mr Joseph Wadsworth and Thomas Goose of Catterall 16
B Tho Cartmell of Claughton Rebels 16
B William son of Richard Clarkson of Winmarly 17
B Ellen Dr of Anthony Gardner of Wiresdale 19
B George son of Thomas Walker of [illegible] 19
B Richard Fisher of Myerscough 24
B Robt son of Mr [illegible] of Catterall 27

This entry from the parish registers of St. Helen's Churchtown records the burial of three rebels hanged for their part in the rebellion of 1715. (Photograph by permission of the Lancashire Records Office and the vicar of St. Helen's church.)

An entry in the register of deaths at St. Leonard's Church, Walton-le-Dale, reads, "Thomas Coupe, weaver, executed for treason 28th January 1715." (This was the January after the Battle of Preston; the new year then began on March 1st, not January 1st.) Most of the prisoners were sent to a life of slavery in the West Indies. One Liverpool merchant transported over six hundred and was paid one pound for each man shipped.

The leaders of the rebellion were taken to London and tried for treason. As they approached the capital they were met by "multitudes of spectators on foot, on horseback, or in coaches, exclaiming 'No Popish Pretender! Down with the rebels. Long live King George!' " It was also reported that as the prisoners were taken in chairs through the streets of London there was a "great outcry" of patriotism towards the Hanoverian regime.

Tom Forster showed more determination in saving his own skin than he had as a military leader. While his master was imprisoned at Newgate, Forster's servant managed to take a wax impression of the gaol's master key and secretly had a duplicate made. Then the general invited the prison governor to dine with him and plied him with strong wine (prisoners then were allowed to eat and drink what they chose so long as they could pay for the luxuries). When the governor became drowsy

Forster sent his servant out for more wine and, when he didn't come back after a long time, Forster made the excuse of going to find him, used the duplicate key to lock the wine-fuddled governor in his cell, and managed to escape to France.

Other leaders of the rebellion were not so fortunate. The Earl of Derwentwater and several others were beheaded. Of the Lancashire leaders, Ralph Standish of Borwick Hall, Albert Hodgson of Leighton and John Dalton of Thurnham all received long prison sentences and were eventually released after paying enormous fines which left their families poor for generations. After his release, John Dalton, once one of the greatest landowners in the north of Lancashire, walked over 250 miles back to his ancestral home at Thurnham near Lancaster, to find it practically in ruins. When he met his wife collecting sticks for her fire they failed at first to recognise each other; privation and suffering had changed them both so much.

So even those Jacobites who escaped death as a punishment for rising against the Hanoverian regime were reduced to a state where they had neither the wealth nor, in most cases, the strength to join again in a military rising. The Hanoverians, unpopular as they were, were secure on the throne of England and it was thirty years before there was another attempt to restore the Stuarts.

2 Bonnie Prince Charlie and the Jacobites march through Lancashire in 1745

THE last ill-fated attempt to restore the Stuart dynasty took place in 1745. Once again it was promise of support from France that made the rebellion possible. England and France were at war (the War of the Austrian Succession) and the king of France took advantage of his chance to embarrass the king of England by encouraging the Jacobites to rebel.

Prince Charles Edward, son of James the Old Pretender, landed at Arisaig with only seven men in 1745. The handsome and brave "Bonnie Prince Charlie" stirred the imagination of the Highland chiefs when he declared, "I, Charles Stuart, have come to claim the crown of my ancestors, or perish in the attempt." The Highlanders flocked to join the prince when he raised his standard at the head of the lonely Loch Shiel and to join him on the march to Edinburgh which he entered in triumph with pipes playing and banners flying. At Prestonpans the rebels' first encounter with Government troops sent to oppose them lasted only five minutes. The claymores and battle-axes of the Highlanders struck terror into the Hanoverians and particularly into the cowardly heart of their leader, General Cope, who was one of the first to flee from the scene of the battle.

In Scotland this triumph for the Jacobites made many more join their victorious ranks. In London the government received the news amidst consternation. King George's son, the Duke of Cumberland, was given command of the reinforced Government troops converging in the Midlands to stop the Jacobites in their march south. General Wade with more troops made for Northumberland, and Newcastle was defenced against possible attack.

But it was through Cumberland, not Northumberland, that Prince Charlie entered England. By November 17th he had entered Carlisle and, leaving behind a garrison to hold that town, the Jacobites marched over Shap Fell to Kendal and so to Lancaster. This time there was no tumultuous welcome for the rebels. When James III was once more proclaimed in the Market Square most of the people of Lancaster went about

The house in Church Street, Lancaster, where Bonnie Prince Charlie stayed in 1745.

their business and remained aloof from the rebels. The prince stayed the night in a house in Church Street (now used as the Conservative Club). Some of the Lancashire Jacobites came there to welcome the prince, but there were few families left who had the means or inclination to support what they considered to be a lost cause. The 1715 rebellion had left many families destitute; they had suffered too much to be willing or able to support this new attempt.

One of those who met at the house in Church Street where the prince stayed the night was Henry Bracken, a well-known Lancaster doctor. While professing to support the Jacobite cause, Dr. Bracken was in fact a staunch supporter of the Hanoverians and even as he discussed plans of campaign with the prince and his advisers he was planning to betray all their schemes. The next morning, just as the main body of the army moved off, the rearguard of the rebels, wearied with the march through the dismal November mists of north Lancashire, trudged into Lancaster. There was no rest for them. According to one writer there was only time for them "to eat bread and cheese in the streets" before they were on the march again – to Preston. The army did not linger here to be beguiled by the beautiful ladies of that town and waste precious time in "courting and feasting." At Preston the prince slept at the home of a local lawyer, Nicholas Starkie. The house in Market Street, afterwards known as "The Palace," has now been demolished.

The Jacobites planned to march south via Wigan and Warrington but their plans had to be changed because the bridge at Warrington had been pulled down as part of a plan to stop the advance of the rebels. The new route chosen was through Manchester. Of the Jacobite troops and their leader in Manchester, we have an account in the diary of "Beppie" Byrom, daughter of John Byrom (it was as a Christmas present for another of his daughters, Dorothy, that John Byrom wrote the famous hymn "Christians Awake"). The Byroms lived in Manchester and Beppie's diary covers the period of the Jacobite rebellions. On August 14th, 1745, she writes, "Great talk of the Pretender coming." By September 26th fear of the Jacobites had prompted the Manchester Presbyterians to send "everything that valuable away – wives, children and all." During November, Beppie records rumours about the insurgents – "an express has come that the rebels are coming, and another that they are not, and so on." By November 25th when the Jacobites had reached Lancaster she reports, "Today there are men pulling up Warrington Bridge. A letter from Penrith says the rebels are but 7,000 men but other accounts say there are 25,000 or 30,000."

By the following day fear of the approaching rebels reported to be at Preston had driven most families away from Manchester. "Everybody is going out of town and sending all their effects away," writes the young diarist, "there is hardly any family left but ours and our kin . . . all the warehouses in the town almost are empty; tonight the bellman is going about to forbid anybody sending provisions out of the town, for a great many have today. Dr. Mainwaring says the rebels have done nothing but what a rabble without a head might have done. They have pulled up Stockport Bridge and Barton Bridge and we expect every minute they will begin at Salford Bridge [they have begun at Cross Street]; if they do some folk say they will set the fire bells off ringing to raise a mob to stop them."

By the following day Beppie had received news of the Prince at Preston and writes, "We expect a party of them (the rebels) here tomorrow. The Prince lay at Lawyer Starkie's at Preston last night; he has marched from Carlisle at the head of his army; he was dressed in a Scotch plaid, a blue silk wistcoat with silver lace and a Scotch bonnet with J.R. on it."

Beppie's prediction was right for on the next day the first of the rebels arrived in Manchester – a serjeant, a drummer and a "spritely girl"! The romantic lure of the white cockade and the promise of a five guinea bounty attracted about thirty recruits before the next contingent of a hundred horsemen arrived to arrange quarters for the main body of the army. Next day, November 29th, Prince Charles Edward arrived in Manchester at the head of an army of about 10,000 men. The prince stayed the night in Market Street Lane and in honour of the royal visitor bonfires were lit and church bells rang out. The excitement of the occasion is conveyed in Beppie Byrom's diary entry for November 30th:

"I dressed me up in my white gown and went up to my aunt Brearcliffe's and an officer called on us to go see the Prince; we went to Mr. Fletcher's and saw him (the Prince) get on horseback, and a noble sight it is. I would not have missed it for a great deal of money; his horse had stood an hour in the court without stirring and as soon as he got on he began a-dancing and capering as he was proud of his burden, and when he rid out of the court he was received with as much joy and shouting almost as if he had been king without any dispute, indeed I think scarce anybody that saw him could dispute it."

Altogether between two and three hundred men had joined the rebels in Manchester and, with Francis Towneley in command, became known as "The Manchester Regiment." From Manchester the Jacobite army of over 10,000 men, 100 laden horses, 16 cannon and numerous covered wagons moved off southwards. The wrecking of the bridges over the Mersey did not stop them. It is reported that Prince Charles Edward forded the river at Stockport leading his army waist deep in the water. Rafts were improvised for the transport of supplies and undeterred the army marched towards Derby. It seemed quite feasible that this army, well disciplined and organised, could reach London. There had been very little resistance to the rebels as they had marched through Lancashire. Sir Henry Hoghton, the Hanoverian campaigner of 1715, had once again offered his services. He wrote to Pelham, the Prime Minister of the time, "You are kind in remembering the part I played then [1715]. I am the same now, only thirty years older, and am still ready to venture my life and my fortune for my King and country." The militia raised by Hoghton had been able to do little apart from keeping guns and ammunition from the rebels.

As the Jacobites pressed on to Derby there was panic in London. Shops closed and citizens rushed to the banks to withdraw their money for fear of the consequences if the rebels reached the capital. The Jacobites, however, never reached London for just when it seemed that the tide of his fortunes was highest, the prince was persuaded, very much against his will, to turn back. His advisers feared that the rebels might be trapped between the forces of General Wade converging on them from Yorkshire and the Duke of Cumberland's forces mustered near Lichfield. Once the decision to retreat had been made there was no hope of victory for the Jacobites, though it is very probable that if they had continued their march the rebellion could have been crowned with success, especially as the promised help was on its way.

The prince, who had marched so proudly at the head of his army, refused to lead the retreat. Instead he rode, a sad and dejected figure, at the back of his troops. He realised that he had made the wrong decision in accepting the advice of his council, and declared, "In future I shall summon no more councils, since I am accountable to nobody for my actions, but to God and my father and therefore I shall no longer ask or accept advice."

By December 9th the retreating army was back in Manchester where, seizing an elderly citizen, James Bayley, as hostage, they demanded and exacted a large sum under threat of sacking the town. The rebels were closely followed by the Duke of Cumberland and his forces. Beppie Byrom refers to Government troops in Manchester when she writes on December 12th, "My brother came and fetched me to see the Duke. We all went up to Aunt Brearcliffe's, stayed there all day but saw nothing but the light horse and hussars which went straight through the town."

Ahead of the duke the rebels entered Lancaster, and there they sought revenge, particularly on two men – Dr. Bracken, who had betrayed their trust in him, and Dr. Fenton, the Lancaster vicar and justice of the peace who had preached vehemently against their cause, and who had punished the rebels captured in the two rebellions. On their march south the rebel army had been well disciplined and there were few complaints of looting and lawlessness. A letter written a few days after the disappointed Jacobites passed through Lancaster on their return march tells a different story:

"The rebels in their passage thro' this town last week behaved like a Parcel of the most consummate villains, the meanest part of them pilfered and stole everything portable for their purpose, and their Chiefs sent Ruffians to plunder and extort money in a most brutal manner from Gentlemen who had exerted themselves most against them. A party of them went to Dr. Fenton's the vicar of this Town, who committed all the outrages their malice suggested. The Doctor was fled from the Vicarage but they presented Pistols and drawn swords – to the breasts and heads of his servants and caused every Room, Chest, Drawer and Box in the House to be opened or broke open, out of which they took what they pleased, and then swore most vehemently that they would burn the house unless £20 was paid to redeem it. This so terrified the Old Lady in the House that she advanced that Sum in Behalf of the Doctor. No sooner had they got the money but they bid the Doctor's servant tell him that they would shoot him through the head whenever they met with him, for they were well informed he was the Greatest Enemy they had in Lancashire, by his frequent preaching against them and intimidating and restraining their friends as a Justice of the Peace."

Dr. Bracken, the traitor, had also taken the precaution of fleeing from Lancaster rather than face retribution at the hands of the rebels who had to content themselves with wreaking their vengeance on his house.

It is not surprising that on this occasion the ladies (and gentlemen as well) were not sorry to see the Jacobites go. All over Lancashire relief was felt when at last the rebels left the county, and jubilation was particularly evident among the non-conformists who had no love for the Stuarts. Beppie Byrom describes unpleasant scenes as the Manchester Presbyterians rejoiced as the vanquished rebels retreated to Scotland:

"The Presbyterians made two effigies of the Prince, one in his Scots dress and one in his English dress, and carried them up and down the town and raised a great mob which was headed by some of the great Presbyterian gentlemen . . . they were very rude and they carried their bundle of rags down to